Girl, Get Out o

Breaking Free to Get and Stay on Track

Dionne Jude
and
Niasha Toole Keens-Douglas

First published in June 2020

Dionne Michelle Jude and Niasha Toole Keens-Douglas assert the moral right to be identified as the authors of this work.

A catalogue record of this book is available from the British Library.

Printed and bound internationally via Amazon KDP

ISBN: 9798657004458

We dedicate this book to our daughters with love and light

Dejai, Alicia and Christa

We also thank the women who have contributed and shared their stories, so that others may overcome as they have done and continue to do xxxxxxxx

Contents

Introduction

Chapter 1
How to know you are getting in your way - 11

Chapter 2
Why are you getting in your way? - 23

Chapter 3
The Girl Getters Mindset - 37

Chapter 4
Girl Getters Inventory Tools - 52

Chapter 5
Tips to get out of your way – 76

Notes

Stories written by

Zephorah Nuré

Evolve or Die – 18

Dr Yvette Ankrah

Purpose from pain – 20

Djennicia Francis

Do It for Spite - 31

Nicole Freeman-Kirkland

Til My Death Do We Part – 34

Dr Gwen Martin

Complacency Impedes Progression – 46

Marchell Coleman

There is No Success in Playing it Safe - 49

LaShartey Mcghee

My Dream, My Purpose - 70

Cindy Mollineau

Surviving the Relationship – 72

Hermilyn Marryshow

Leaving Paradise – 96

Sarah Shard

Self-care is a Self Must – 99

Introduction

This book is for women who know that they are getting in their own way and want to do something about it. We are writing as your sister and a dear friend, that person who gives you the right advice at the right time. We call these women Girl Getters, women who are wanting to achieve something no matter how big or small, significant or impactful. This could be something in their lives, in their homes, with a partner, for their kids, at work or in business.

Their intention is clear, their passion is strong, but they don't always follow through. We know, because we have been in the same position and on some days or for periods of time, we go through the same routine of wanting something, sometimes starting, but never fully executing to get the results we desire. We can only write this book because we have also been in a place of allowing our personal barriers, lack of confidence and limiting beliefs to hold us back.

We are the mothers, wives, single women, entrepreneurs, sisters, the colleagues alike and one thing is clear, we are no longer prepared to settle or get in our own way. In this book we provide a simple, honest, yet thoughtful look at the reasons why women tend to get in their own way in chapter 1.

Chapter 2 explores why women get in their way, exploring fear as a primary cause and personal barrier to our success.

Chapter 3 outlines what we consider the 'Girl Getters' mindset - the values, beliefs, attitudes and behavioural habits that drives and motivates us to take the action.

Chapter 4 provides an inventory to assist you to take a good look at yourself and what is going on below the surface.

Chapter 5 outlines some key tips and resources that can enable you to make the necessary changes needed.

At the end of each chapter you will find inspirational stories of women, written in their own words. We feel honoured to share their heart-felt stories with you and trust you can relate to their individual journeys that they now stand triumphant over.

Chapter 1

How to Know You Are Getting in Your Way

There are various things that we do to get in our way and each of us has a different strategy. We have listed a few ideas below that you might be familiar, but others may come as a surprise, as they happen at an unconscious level. Read through the following and give yourself a grade, based on how much you have done each one.

0 = I have not done this
3 = I do this sometimes
5 = I do this all the time

Not getting things done - You have a list and you know there are things you need to complete, yet they stay on your list or in your mind. What you want to complete stays unfinished and there are times that you don't start at all. Are you putting off writing that book or starting that business; delaying clearing out the closest or tidying up the cupboard that is brimming with old stuff; or are you running away from having a difficult conversation, that is important but necessary.

Making excuses - You may have reasons why you think things are not happening for you and some of these things are out of your control. However, there are times when you are just making excuses for yourself, hoping they will cover up for your lack of action. Excuses get in your way and can prevent you from having a good look at your personal barriers and unconscious drivers. Excuses like, it's not the right time, not having enough money, not knowing where to start, not having enough support, looking after the kids, it's the fault of the pandemic etc. Remember there will always be a reason why you can't do something, your responsibility, is to find a way to make it happen.

Not getting results - You want to achieve something and you might have a clear idea in your mind about what it looks like, but by getting in your own way you do not get the results you so desire This often looks like, a business not hitting targets or growing as much as you would like, failing to meet financial goals, not losing the weight or reaching your health goals. It can be disheartening when we don't get the outcome we so wanted, and this can dent our motivation.

Getting undesirable results - Sometimes you get results that you don't want, and this may be because of not taking action, or not doing the correct thing. Having a healthy balance so you are being efficient – getting the right results verse being effective – working on the right things is crucial. We don't always get want we want in life, however, there are ways that we contribute to things not turning out the way we would like. Attracting douche-bag boyfriends or the same type of partner over and over despite affirming you want something different, health problems caused by an unhealthy lifestyle, not passing tests, exams or an appraisal because you didn't put the time in. Taking the wrong type of action can be just as damaging as taking no action at all.

Slow or no change - Change happens, and is happening around us all the time, whether we like it or not. There may be some things that you would like to change in your life, but it is not happening, or you might be making slow progress. Did you think you would be married, with child, had several children or divorced by now? Or did you think you would be over that person or situation, but it seems to be taking a long time? When things take a long time to change, we can become disheartened. But sticking in there may be what is needed, and you may be closer than you think.

Ignoring the signs - You are taking action and things might not be going the way you would like. There are key indicators that things are not working out and are not going the way you would like. Ignoring these signs can be detrimental, especially if you don't adjust or respond to before it's too late. Ignoring the pains, not going to the doctor before things get worse, not addressing the first time someone showed you disrespect and then being surprised when it happens again, wearing those rosy coloured glasses, which taint your view of someone when you first meet them, so you ignore when they don't keep their word or keep letting you down. It might seem easier to look the other way, but unfortunately, what you choose not to see, or address might come back to bite you.

Recurring patterns and cycles - You have been down the road before, so you know exactly where it will take you, hoping things will be different next time. You are familiar with the outcomes and almost feel resigned to what you think is going to happen. Despite knowing the patterns, you may be unsure how to prevent them from happening again and again. How many times have you said you are going to save money and not spend it on that dress or makeup etc. but you end up broke at the end of the month again? Or dieting for the fourth time in two years, losing a bit of weight but then putting it on again until the next time. Make a choice to end these cycles, especially when they are not adding to your life.

Putting things off - Procrastination is a classic sign of getting in your way, however it is not always easy to spot. Before you know it, you are tucked up in bed or doing your favourite thing, while what you are putting off is waiting to be done in the side lines. Saying you will get to it another day or next week, has become your favourite pastime, and sometimes to your detriment you never do. Before you know it, years have passed you by, while your purpose awaits.

Lacking energy - This can happen because of not being motivated or when feeling unwell. When we feel motivated and inspired it's amazing where we find the energy to do the things we want to do. Unless you have a health condition, lacking energy may be down to a lack of motivation for what you need to do. It's important that you discover the whys and reasons behind what you are doing. For example, are you studying because your parents thought it might be a good idea? Are you working in a particular industry because you thought it might make you look good, but secretly despise your job every day?

Doing what you love - It's great to put time and energy into what you love. However, this can get in the way, especially when we spend time on what we enjoy (which has its place), rather than what we supposed to be doing. This often leaves the important and sometimes urgent tasks left undone, while we unconsciously sabotage our success, even though we are in our flow. For example, if you enjoy helping people, you might dedicate a lot of time doing this, rather than building a sustainable business.

Putting others first - As a result of our female caring and nurturing tendencies, we are likely to put the needs of others before our own. No doubt you have important roles to fulfil, dedicating time to making sure others are ok. But what about you? When on a plane when there is a problem the pilot always urges people to put their seatbelt on first, before assisting others, this even includes helping a child or an elderly person. Parents often have a tough time with this one, and some put their lives on hold until their children grow up. Now there is nothing wrong with this, but it can be difficult when you have dreams and passions that are not being fulfilled.

Not showing up - On some days, it is okay to relax, do nothing and chillax, however, this is different from being lazy. Being lazy prevents you from showing up for the things that are waiting to be done. Showing up looks like putting pen to paper, so you finish that assignment or book, doing the small things that will help you to reach your targets and goals, and keeping your word to others doing the things you said you would do. When you don't show up others may lose their faith and trust in you – placing you as someone that can't be relied one.

Self-sabotage - Things seem to be going well, you are making progress and then boom! You do something to throw you off track or derail things altogether. This is often linked to an unconscious fear of success or failure (to be explored in the next chapter) which makes you think or do things has an impact on you. Self-sabotage is rarely a conscious thing and can be driven by previous experiences that you do not wish to replicate. For example, being rejected by someone you have a connection with.

Imposter syndrome - You are in a place that you have earned and others believe in you and what you can achieve, but you don't believe in yourself. It doesn't matter how you got there, what is important is how you stay there and thrive. Lacking confidence in yourself and your abilities leads you to focus more on what is going on in your inner world, rather than taking action in your outer world. Did you work hard to get a promotion, but feel scared about meeting expectations? Have you started a new relationship, but fear them discovering the real you? Have you started a new business that looks good on social media, but you worry about people finding out how things really are?

Being overly busy -You can be very busy and still not get what you need to get done started or finished. Busyness is an excellent way to put things off, as it make you feel like you are taking action, but it could be that you are not taking action in regards to the things that really matter. Busyness can be an excellent time thief, as by the time you catch yourself, hours and days have gone by.

Zephorah's Story

Evolve or Die!

The journey to "getting out of my own way" began when I created a successful aphrodisiac spa line called the Hawaiian Spa Beauty and Bath Collection from Nuré Spa. The bath line is centred around self - care and consists of Hydra-Silk Body Lotion, Silky Body Oil, Luxury Bubble Bath, Sugar Scrub, Face Masques, and Aphrodisiac Tea. I created this concept after a career as a model that spanned for over 15 years and having found the perfect beauty system for women to achieve flawless skin. The idea came to me after a solo trip to the enchanted islands of Hawaii. The intent was to gift-wrap the serene tropical feeling into a beautiful box for the women of NYC who needed self-care after a long day of work and the harsh life that comes with living in a big city. My ultimate dream was to be able to create the lifestyle I want – to build a thriving bath and beauty line that allowed me to travel and give inspirational speeches. However, I knew that the only way to achieve this goal was to leave The Big Apple behind along with its distractions such as having an unfulfilling day job and slaving to pay expensive rent to maintain a certain lifestyle.

I procrastinated on leaving because I feared what awaited me on the other side. After a while, I began hearing my inner voice screaming at me to leave NYC because it was time for me to fulfil my purpose. And if I continued to stay, I could have made myself sick or even died, because I was not growing. Evolve or Die is a real thing. One day, I went to the doctor, and she thought I had cancer, even though she could not officially diagnose me. I didn't take it seriously because I knew deep down in my heart, I didn't have it – it was a scare, and this was God's final warning. The doctors finally informed me that I didn't have cancer, but I knew that it was time to go. At last, I moved out of the city and back to my hometown in Ohio to be rid of distractions and pursue my dream.

Now that I left New York, I am out of my own way and fully immersed and flourishing with the Hawaiian Spa Beauty and Bath Collection. I can travel to places like Atlanta, California, Orlando, and many other areas to give talks and introduce my line. I also mentor young women who want to begin a career in modelling. I really wish I would have done this sooner but better late than never! I am living my true purpose.

One thing I've learned, whenever you have big dreams, sacrifices will have to be made. It is truly a wilderness when you strike out on your own, but the reward is worth it in the end. So, girl, get out of your own way, and just do it!

Yvette's Story

Purpose from pain

Lying in a hospital bed recovering from an unnecessary procedure, was the wake-up call I needed, and I knew that something had to change. That event was the catalyst to a long journey of healing and self-discovery. I learned about the true meaning of self-care the hard way. Years of not listening to my body and pushing and pushing and pushing for success, eventually took its toll. I developed a long-term health condition which left me incapacitated by pain and unable to do things I had taken for granted. There were days I struggled to walk, read or look after my child.

I spent years being an over achiever. I was always going for goals, going above and beyond with everything I did. The first time I experienced burnout was in my 20s, I was working in the corporate environment and on the surface, it seemed that I had an enviable life. The reality was very different, working 12-hour days, not feeling fulfilled and thinking that the occasional weekend away was enough for self-care. These habits and behaviours became ingrained and they the only way I knew how to achieve. When I went into business for myself, I brought those same patterns into my business. However, by now I was older and a mother - the real toll on my health had begun to show. I had to change.

I took time to go within and start addressing what was really going on for me, to look at my relationship with stress and anxiety, and to shift the fear, the stress, the worry and remove things that no longer served me. Removing beliefs and 'truths' I held about and told myself. I believed that I had to work hard all the time, asking for help was a weakness and that I had to prove that I was 'good enough'.

I'm happy to say that I've moved from someone who was burnt out to somebody who is blissed out and pain free. I operate from a space of calm and help others to do the same. I found my purpose and enjoy, who I am, now more than ever.

I invite you to find your calm, to address your fears and to move forward by standing in your strength.

"You may not control all the events that happen to you, but you can decide not to be reduced by them."

Maya Angelou

Chapter 2

Why Are You Getting in Your Way?

Scientists have suggested that humans are born with two fears. The first is a based on a study of depth perception, discovered by in 1960, by J Gibson and R D Walk - they found that humans are born with the fear of falling and S D Norrholm's research found that loud noises are also an innate fear. Thus, fear serves a purpose in our life, but in relation to our goals and achieving our potential, it has no place here. So many people are sitting scared, numbed by the thoughts that scare them and keeps them in their comfort zone and what makes it even more difficult is that this is often an unconscious process. Also, the things we fear often look different on the surface, yet if we take time to explore the deep-rooted reasons, we might find one of the following fears lurking below. These fears can cause us to micro-sabotage daily, even if we are not fully aware of them.

Fear of failure

This is when you worry about not making it or getting the results you desire. The thought of failing can stop you from taking action, leading to not starting a project, increased procrastination, or not finishing things. This the belief that things won't happen to or for you if you try, so why try or take action in the first place?

Social media shows us how wonderful the lives of other people are, yet most only show us what they want us to see. The danger with this is when we start comparing our lives and journey to others, believing that we can't do as well as they are doing, or that they must have a special formula that we don't have that could lead to our demise.

Also, part of this fear could be that you think only good things only happen to other people, that you are not a lucky person, that your religion or the law of attraction doesn't work for you (if you are a believer.) Your life experience to date may make you feel this way and there may have been a lot of things that make you feel scared of trying because from experience you already know the outcome. But if we don't try then we will never know, many people don't give things a go because they do not believe they are worthy or blessed enough. Know that you are enough! Also, be mindful of not being able to see the good that is happening because your mindset is always focused on looking for the bad, the failings and tragedy.

When there is something that you want to achieve, it's difficult to know if it will happen for you. The fear of failure can make people anxious about putting in the effort to achieve a specific outcome, because they feel that they might not get anything out of it. No action, equal no wasted effort.

Fear of success

This type of fear is less well known as the fear of failure. This is when people worry about what will happen because of achieving the goals and outcomes they desire. For example, what will happen if I find the partner of my dreams? Will I have to give up my freedom or sacrifice my career? You might be anxious about not having enough time to relax or do what you love – believing success takes hard work, sacrifice and commitment. This is fear of the unknown and not knowing what to expect when you make it.

Sometimes women fear making it big, as they are worried about what other people will say, especially if they start living a different lifestyle. Family and friends might start to treat you differently, or colleagues may become envious if you get that promotion. You remember the remarks and conversations you had with them about other successful people or achieving something they haven't, and this could put you off. For example, some people say, "she is showing off", "she doesn't know nobody now she has made it", "who does she think she is" etc.

Another aspect of this type of fear is worry that once you make it, it will all be taken away from you. This is a very real fear for women who have experienced loss or rejection in their lives. So, the thought about reaching for something more, scares the heaven out of some women based on what has happened in the past.

Fear of change

Some women worry about how things will be different, the fear of change is also a fear of the unknown. Even if life will be better and there is a possibility of being happier and more at peace, some of use choose not the take action that could lead to transformation, simply because unconsciously we are comfortable with the life we are leading. Any type of change is guaranteed to push you beyond your comfort zone, and when things start to become uncomfortable, you might choose to retreat to a space and more familiar space. The unfortunate thing about this is that growth can't happen if you are not prepared to experience uncomfortable times, that potentially take you away from the safety and security of the life you are leading, even if you are unhappy. For example, not knowing who you will become, if you will be accepted, how different will your life be and who or what will you outgrow.

Humans are creatures of habit, and these unconscious behaviours assist us by preventing us from having to learn new things each time we encounter a specific situation, however the detrimental side to our habits is when we engage in behaviour that does not allow us to move forward, keeping us in places and spaces that we wish to break free from, but our unchallenged unconscious drivers keep shaping our thoughts, feelings, words and actions in a way that holds us back.

Change will not happen if you are not prepared to venture beyond what you know and you are not expected to take massive leaps, only to start putting one foot in front of the other, small steps towards what you truly desire.

Fear of the what is missing

Working as a breakthrough coach enabled Dionne to develop a key understanding, of the common denominators that prevent people from moving forward. One of the things she picked up was the sense that her clients felt something was missing. Dionne began referring to this as the void, to symbolise this common experience. The void is a sense that something is missing - as human beings we spend a lot of time doing stuff, rather than being. Human 'doings' would have been a better name for us. Pre-occupying our time, keeping busy, going non-stop, being a workaholic enables us to not feel the gap that exists within all of us.

Imagine that this gap, is a space that exists within all of us, as a valuable space that we can experience a great sense of peace. For those that are religious or spiritual the gap, can be considered a place that contains the All-That-Is, a space that a being greater than ourselves exists or can enter to be with us. But we are often too busy to take the time to allow this to happen. We would like to challenge you to imagine that the void is necessary and that taking time to enter it and be okay with it, is a crucial part of developing inner peace, joy and happiness, regardless of what is going on in our world. Let it be ok that you feel empty, sometimes, but know that rather than feeling lack this is a powerful time to embrace the fullness of who you truly are. Being left alone with our own thoughts and feelings can be scary.

We are all guilt of reaching out for void-fillers. These are things that prevent us from feeling loneliness, worthless or that we don't have a purpose for being. Food, alcohol, sex, work, gossip, unhealthy TV, obsessively going to the gym and anything else that we do in extremes. All these things can be an attempt to replace unwanted thoughts and feelings.

What do you fill the void with?

How do you feel when you are left alone with your thoughts and feelings?

Acknowledging that you have a void is important, however taking time to enter and be at peace with the feelings that the void can evoke can be challenging. There are some good ways that we can get inside the void, so we can have a positive experience.

Four truths about fear

Susan Jeffers, in her book Feel the Fear and Do It Anyway, suggests there are several truths that can help us to see far for what it is. Susan shares an acronym for fear, false evidence appearing real and recognising fear for what it is and pushing past it can bring a sense of relief. Here are the 4 truths about fear according to Susan Jeffers.

1. *'The fear will never go away as long as you continue to grow'*

Accept that fear is a part of your life, especially if you are on a journey and aspire to do something different or worthwhile. If you are committed to your personal or professional growth expect to feel some sort of fear almost on a daily sis. Thus, it's important to be aware of this, acknowledge the fear and thank it for being present as it is a sign that you are growing.

2. *'The only way to get rid of the feat of doing something is to go out and...do it!'*

Susan Jeffers acronym for fear – false evidence appearing real. So, one of the ways to be able to move beyond fear is realising that what you fear may not be as big or as bad as you believe it to be. Secondly, only by taking action will you start to see that it is not as bad as you thought in the first place. Finally, once you have conquered the fear by taking action, it no longer has such a hold over your life.

3. *'The only way to feel better about yourself is to go out and...do it!'*

Imagine how you will feel about yourself when you get to the other of fear. Hopefully, you will be able to give yourself a big pat on the back and may receive positive feedback from other. Even if you are not good at receiving praise, acknowledge how brave you have been and the courage you have amassed to help you achieve your goal.

4. *'Not only are you afraid when facing the unknown, so is everyone else'*

   It's fair to say that everyone has a fear of some-thing. You are not alone in feeling fear or at getting in your own way. We may all have our different reasons and it can seem quite lonely at times, but you are not the only one that goes through this. Also, you have strengths where someone's fear starts and helping others is a good way of developing your confidence.

Djennicia's Story
Do It for Spite!

This story goes back to Whitney Houston's "I'm Not Afraid to Try" ... the most afraid rendition in human history. I was a spitfire of a child. Talented, brilliant and opinionated; cocooned in crippling stage fright and an ever-prevailing fear of failure! Just imagine the cognitive dissonance. Now, throw in being dark skinned with short hair in a society that lauds lighter complexions and straight or mixed long hair. The night of the infamous rendition, I'd volunteered to sing as my solo debut in a church function. I'd expected stage presence, spotlights, a talent extravaganza! I gave, barely audible, shivering mannequin. COGNITIVE DISSONANCE!

However, the stage called and I kept answering, poorly. Seriously, I forgot our national anthem, on stage.... As I moved into adolescence however, I realized that I was afraid A LOT. I said "no" to outings, opportunities, adventures and Just. Being. me, because I was afraid. Precocious as I was, I decided "Enough is Enough!" No more living a half-life due to fear. I promised myself that I would "Do it Afraid." Every time an opportunity presented itself, I had something to say or wanted to try, I would ask myself "Is fear the only thing keeping back?" If the answer was yes, I would do it for spite.

I climbed cliffsides that fell men, spoke up in choir practice, though it was never well received, and, finally, did good solo performances. My mom relaxed my hair and as sad as it is, that helped also. Then came Cotillion, a competition, with every girl I was insecure around and usually looked over for! But I remembered, and, yes, fear was the only thing holding me back, so I did it, for spite. And. I. WON! Cognitive Dissonance, dissipating!

Then, I ventured into Pageantry! I stepped on my first pageant stage in 2013 and came 3rd. Cognitive Dissonance dissipating. 2014, my first pageant win. Dissonance dissipating. By 2016, a couple days after my 25th birthday, which was June 25th, I won the most prestigious pageant in the Caribbean, Miss Carnival. A competition that my country had not won in 25 years.

Today, I am a Queen multiple times over, slaying before thousands. A professional Master of Ceremonies. and Pageant Coach whose client just won the Face-of-Grenada. A worship leader, Spoken Word artist, Speech Writer and Public Speaking Coach, teaching others to make their voices heard. OH and I. Have. Gone. Confidently. Natural. Dissonance dumped!

Ladies, with every new venture, I'm usually afraid to try, but I've learned that the greater the fear, the more it means to me. So, I do it for spite. I "Do it Afraid" and I am living proof that the confidence WILL come.

It is your duty to match your reality to all that your heart and mind are telling you, you should be.

I invite you on my journey to teach children to Master their Minds so they can Master their realities, in my first, yes, I am terrified, Children's Book "In the Mirror."

Nicole's Story
Til My Death Do We Part

Marriage is a sacred contract between two people, we say our vows, make a promise to love each other through sickness and in health, to forsake all others as long as we both shall live. So, if this were true, then why was I so unhappy, why was I looking for everything else to fill the void within me? From the outside it looked like I had everything, a great husband, my best friend, and 8 years of building our family. I often tell myself, if I had to do it all over again, it would be different. I would get out of my own way sooner. Here I was married to a man that I loved but was not in love with, I was pretending that everything was okay, and it was not. At the weakest point in my first marriage, it got so bad that I began to search outside for people, things, and places to fill the void. Even now I think about my past mistakes in love, what did I really gain from making poor choices that ultimately led to many years of pain and suffering? But as time would tell, I would make the choice to walk away from what was not working, into a much worse circumstance. I was in my own way and did not realize it until it was almost too late.

I left a loveless marriage for an abusive marriage. I was running in cycles of self-defeat, creating negative patterns in relationships that were toxic and unhealthy. I was always on an emotional rollercoaster.

In my second marriage I encountered abuse on many levels, emotional, mental, and physical, I had become a victim of domestic violence. At the age of 43 I already had two failed marriages under my belt. I knew deep down inside things had to change.

One day after a physical altercation with my husband, I looked into the eyes of my 3-year-old daughter, and it was that moment I had to say to myself enough is enough. Yes, I was afraid to leave, domestic violence relationships are so unpredictable, you never know what will happen. I had no real plan, no money, and my youngest child to protect.

Here I was preparing to leave yet another failed marriage. To say I was terrified does not give it justice, but I had to believe that life was going to get better on the other side, I made up in my mind that failure was not an option. I swallowed my pride, sought help from a friend, I made a fresh start on January 4, 2015 and I never looked back. Starting over was not easy, but it was necessary. I began to love myself and life again. I refocused my dreams on my career, I was able to grow my business and attract a six-figure revenue stream. I accomplished many of my goals, and through it all I met and married a wonderful man, where the love is mutual, we see each other as the best version of ourselves.

"There is a stubbornness about me that can never bear to be frightened at the will of others. My courage always rises at every attempt to intimidate me."

Jane Austen

Chapter 3

The Girl Getters Mindset

The 14 Commandments

Women who take action and get things done have a growth mindset. Carol Dweck spoke about the difference between having a fixed mindset and growth mindset, as the difference between believing you can't change (fixed) verse believing you can grow and change by learning (growth.) Having a growth mindset is important to getting out of your way and getting what you want. Here are some of the beliefs will assist you with being a girl getter.

A girl getter is a female who…

1. **I have a can-do attitude and I am determined to do what it takes to get what I desire**

- Believe that you can do what you need to do, or at least have the willpower to find out how.
- Develop a kick-ass determination to succeed because you know that you will do what it takes to get ahead

2. **I take time to be clear about what I desire and my goals - I know the direction I am going in**

- Know what you want and the reasons why you want them
- Set SMART goals, so you have clear outcomes and objectives
- Know what success looks like, so you know when you get there
- Use this to get focused so you direct your time and energy in the right way

3. I may feel scared sometimes, but I keep going despite lacking courage

- It's ok to feel the fear, recognise it for what it is, but don't allow it to paralyze you and stop you
- Being courageous does not mean you will not be scared, but that you will take action regardless of the fear
- Remember everyone feels fear and is not confident about everything - keep taking action despite the fear

4. I have my off days and know it's okay as everyone goes through this

- Having down time is important and you should not beat yourself up about it. Take time off when you need to recharge and refuel.
- Everyone has down days when they don't feel like doing anything. Beating yourself up for feeling this way, just makes you feel worse.

- Rest and relaxation strengthen you for the days when you take massive action

5. **I live an authentic life, being myself and doing what I really want to do**

- It's okay to shine and be yourself, even though many women are given the opposite message
- Our families, media, religion, education etc. through the process of socialisation have taught us direct and indirect messages about the women they believe we should become. Because we grew up with these ideas, many of us do not question them and this can affect how we would like to live our lives

6. **Balance is important to me and I will find ways to develop all areas of my life**

- Many women who are living busy lives, lack a balanced approach to their work, family life, relationships and well-being. Having balance can be quite challenging, however, it's important to do what you can to take time to nurture each area.
- Knowing what needs to be developed, starts by conducting an inventory of these areas of life e.g. wheel of life process. This gives you ideas about what you need to work on or what you are ignoring.

7. **I learn from mistakes and choose to do better next time**

- We all make mistakes, but the key is to not keep making the same mistake, because you are not taking time to grow or say no.
- Iyanla Vanzants says 'you are going to be a fool, you just need to decide how many times you are going to be a fool…'
- Hindsight and reflection are our friends; so when you make mistakes put some time aside to think about what you could have done differently.

8. **I invest in myself, knowing that I am my greatest asset**

- How much time have you spent investing in others? Investing in yourself requires you to know what you need to learn and find ways to develop your skills and knowledge
- There are many online courses and books that are dedicated to personal development, which are free or you can purchase. There are various priced resources, but the money that you spend is an investment in yourself and your future.

9. **I have a superpower that I work to develop, I build on my strengths and work on the areas that require development**

- Everyone has a superpower, which is something that they do well. This is a skill that you have that you do better than anyone else.
- Continue to hone your superpower; find ways to put it to practice,
- Remember your strength, might be someone's weakness, so find people you can share your skills with

10. I take inspired action and finds ways to get motivated, so I am driven when I need to be

- There are days when you don't feel like doing anything and need something to motivate you.
- Think about the things that make you feel inspired, that give you a boost and make you feel better quickly. This can be music, motivational videos, affirmations, conversation with a friend or family m
- When you feel driven you can feel unstoppable and those are the days to get things done, when you feel energised

11. I care about others and I am never too busy to take time to connect with them

- Take time to connect with those you care about, to see how they are doing. Sometimes when we are busy, we forget to check in and they might not say something to us, but they might feel neglected, even thought that is not your intention.

- This is also about letting them know you are okay and need support, not just when you need it, but through a positive relationship, that you are taking time to nurture.

12. I act from a place of integrity and I want others to win just as much as I want it for myself

- The approach of 'by any means necessary', can be motivating, just as long as it is not detrimental to yourself and others.
- The golden rule, inspires us to treat others how we want to be treated, acting from a good place that harms no one.
- When we desire to create win-win solutions, we want great things to happen all around and don't seek to undermined or step on others along the way.

13. I know when to surrender and let go when things get too much or when I feel overwhelmed

- You may get to a place, when you find nothing is working, no matter how much you push forward nothing happens
- This may be the time to surrender, not to the situation completely, but so you can be still for a while, clearing your mind to achieve clarity

- Oprah is a champion of this approach, as she suggests surrendering to a higher power, was instrumental to her success. She sang the song 'I surrender all'
- Think about the things you need to let of and stop doing at this time.

14. I take small steps, one foot in front of the other each day, so I am taking action no matter how small

- No matter how big the task, taking small steps moves you in the right direct.
- There are days when you will take huge strides, but if you hit a stumbling block this might set you back. Be encouraged to take small steps, so not to stop the momentum you have already made.

The 14 Girl Getters Commandments

1) I have a can-do attitude and I am determined to do what it takes to get what I desire.
2) I take time to be clear about what I desire and my goals - I know the direction I am going in
3) I may feel scared sometimes, but I keep going despite lacking courage
4) I have my off days and know it's okay as everyone goes through this
5) I live an authentic life, being myself and doing what I really want to do
6) Balance is important to me and I will find ways to develop all areas of my life
7) I learn from mistakes and choose to do better next time
8) I invest in myself, knowing that I am my greatest asset
9) I have a superpower that I work to develop, I build on my strengths and work on the areas that require development

10) I take inspired action and finds ways to get motivated, so I am driven when I need to be

11) I care about others and I am never too busy to take time to connect with them

12) I act from a place of integrity and I want others to win just as much as I want it for myself

13) I know when to surrender and let go when things get too much or when I feel overwhelmed

14) I take small steps, one foot in front of the other each day, so I am taking action no matter how small

Gwen's Story
Complacency Impedes Progression

Do you have a compilation of great ideas just waiting to be released to the world? Are you a person everyone calls for solutions to problems personally and professionally? Are you the person who motivates others? Are you the calm in the storm of life? Well I am, and this is my story. I am a passionate, hard-working, devoted teacher, counselor, and former college professor. I have dedicated my career to working with some of the most vulnerable, challenging, and high needs populations.

I reached my pinnacle education level in 2009 by earning a doctorate degree in Educational Leadership. I have basked in the success of 20+ years as an educator. My passion is teaching whether it is children, adolescents, or adults. However, over the past few years with the lack of autonomy, increasing role demands and lack of administrative support, I found myself losing that gnawing hunger that initial drove me to the education profession. I realize complacency in doing what I love despite the challenges have kept me rooted in the traditional work setting.

For years, colleagues, supervisors, family, and friends have encouraged me to share my experiences and expertise on a broader platform. It has always been a dream to step out on my own. For years, I procrastinated and made up excuses because I was more comfortable with the status quo. It is easy to get distracted and caught up in the hustle and bustle of daily life, letting too many years go by with little goal progression.

In 2019, I finally stopped settling for being "good enough", took initiative, and started to relentlessly pursue my dream. I allowed my talents to lead to the creation of a new me. I got out of my own way and took the leap into entrepreneurship. I started Dr. Gwen's Counselor Café. I am invested in my goals and am actively striving to make my dream a reality. I now have that fire in my belly again as I work to make the Café a success and my full-time career. I am excited, committed, and motivated. I feel empowered to create change, take calculated risks, break the mould, and add greater value to the world.

I am most passionate about helping others to take care of themselves professionally, physically, psychologically, emotionally, and spiritually. My mission is to support and empower helping professionals, primarily educators, in finding a healthy work/life balance. Self-care is essential to longevity and sustainability. I have learned over the past 23 years that if I do not establish effective self-care, health and wellness routines, the potential for burnout is huge and I want to share that insight with others. I have a plethora of resources, tools, strategies, and ideas that are not only useful but life changing. I am committed to living my best, most authentic life and my goal is to support others in living their best life too.

Marchell's Story
There is No Success in Playing it Safe

Fear, uncertainty, and self-doubt are the feelings I experienced when I was considering the idea of starting my business in 2011. I was suffering from imposter syndrome and low self-confidence about my abilities. Even though I was prepared for my career, I worked hard, went to college, and sacrificed many things in life, I still felt inadequate. For years, I was spinning on the wheels of procrastination, creating lofty goals about starting a business, but doing zero to get me there.

I had no idea how it worked. Back in those days, I did not know much about business coaches or mentors for entrepreneurs. I think in the end, I really did not want to admit the biggest issue for me was, I was the quintessential type A personality and girl perfectionist.

One of the biggest obstacles that held me back for many years, was the fear of rejection. I held onto this idea for years and it kept me in a cycle of false starts and do overs. At times I felt guilty for having such high ambitions, I was doing great in my career, I was able to land good jobs with great pay and benefits. So, why start on this path of entrepreneurship, what did I really have to gain? This was the first mindset shift I had to make on this journey, I also had to qualify the people that I was allowing to speak into my life. The discouragement that others were bringing was not healthy or progressive. Still, I continued to play it safe, kept working full-time, and stopped focusing on my dream and what I believed to be my divine purpose.

At last, I decided in 2014, that I had to get clear about what I genuinely wanted, I had to come to terms with the idea, that I had been conditioned to play it safe, and many of the people in my inner circle were also safe players. I needed to find the exit door fast, I had to get clear. One of the first things I had to do was, find a business coach, mentor or someone who knew more than I did about what it takes to be successful in business. The second thing I had to do was get realistic about my goals and build a foundation. I also had to come to terms with my true fears about success and money. What I discovered on this journey is, those who are called to it, have a special mission in life. I had to accept that my mission in life was much bigger than me, it was part of my divine life path. I got serious and got to work, opening my first business in 2014. My perspective on life was clear, my confidence in myself is stronger than ever, the ultimate lesson for me was, even when you are afraid do something new, do it anyway.

"I'm learning how to drown out the constant noise that is such an inseparable part of my life. I don't have to prove anything to anyone. I only have to follow my heart and concentrate on what I want to say to the world. I run my world."

Beyoncé

Chapter 4

Girl Getters Inventory Tools

Guuuuuuurl, do you know that the only person who can really stop you, is you? Your mindset plays a big role, in shaping your thoughts, feelings, words, actions and what you believe is possible. Before we start looking at the tools that can help you. Let's explore this a little further.

Our thoughts create our feelings, which have an impact on our internal voice and the things we say out loud. Our feelings then direct the actions we take and because this chain reaction happens so quickly, we do not always realise why we have said and done something and what motivated us to do so. Also, because we experience our emotions, more strongly that our thoughts, many of us are directed by our feelings, which is not always a good thing.

Brue Lipton in his book, The Biology of Belief suggests humans are controlled by their emotions - he states that 'the body believes it is in control, when it is actually directed by our thoughts.'

Monitor what you think

Have you ever heard the sayings? "You are what you think" or "Whether you believe you can or you can't you are right". The actions that you take or choose not to take are directed by your dominant thoughts, which have been shaped by your life experiences. Our mind, both conscious and unconscious are the engine rooms of our thoughts, so being in the right mindset is something that is extremely important.

When you think about your dominant thoughts, how much do you think they assist you with your achieving your goals, dreams, visions and desires?

When we are born our minds are a clean slate, a blank canvas, we have no habits, judgments, few fears and we do not know what is right from wrong, according to the society that we are born in to. Babies are like sponges and through the process of socialisation, they grow up living what we they are taught, inheriting and learning habits, both good and bad of those around us. Our habits, thoughts and beliefs are created from what we see and hear in our environment. However, as adults we can create our own thoughts, and with some training the ability to choose what we think and feel. We also can choose to either keep the thoughts and habits that we developed from childhood, or we can learn to start thinking for ourselves. Many of us do not realise that we are still functioning using the thoughts and beliefs that we developed as children. As adults our responsibility is to assess which thoughts have served us well, as these are the ones that can be kept to build our foundation. In the same vein we should also monitor and be aware of the thoughts that hinder us. As these are the ones that have turned into limiting beliefs within our unconscious mind holding us back from living the life that we deserve. Let's take our money mindset for example. If we were raised in a household where money caused fights between our parents, or where they were always struggling to make ends meet. This can lead to you having the same relationship with money. You have the power to change what you think and believe, to suit the person that you are now and choose to become next.

Ways to assess your thoughts

- Listen in on yourself and become conscious of any negative thoughts or limiting beliefs that come to your mind.
- Write a list of your dominant thoughts that you think daily, to review if they are assisting or restricting you, e.g. I am not good enough, they are better than me, I am never going to get there.
- Once you have identified the restrictive or negative thoughts, write out the opposite e.g. change I can't do this, to I can do this if I keep going.
- Keep replacing or reframing the negative thought or limiting belief, until it becomes your dominant thought.

Warning: This is not an overnight process! It takes your commitment and determination over a sustained period.

Monitor what you feel

Like your thoughts you can control the way you feel, even though for some, this takes a lot more effort. Feelings are an energy, emotional state, a vibration, which determines how we react to our thoughts, a person or situation. There are many feelings that we experience as women, i.e. anger, fear, disgust, happiness, sadness, surprise, contempt, depression, joy, excitement and guilt. Just to name a few!

Check your emotions

- What are the dominant emotions that you feel on a regular basis? Especially related to an area of life that you would like to make progress in.
- When you feel these emotions, where do you feel it in your body?
- How do these feelings get in your way of taking action?
- How do these feelings shape what your internal voice and what you say out loud?
- What are the thoughts that cause you to feel this way?

The beauty of it all is that you can take better control of what you feel. You can make improvements in the way you react to your thoughts, other people and situations. There will be times when for one reason or another, we have feelings that don't serve us, like anxiety, fear, sadness or anger. And yes it's ok to have those feelings as we are human after all and being in better control of your feelings, does not mean pretending that you cannot be affected by what happens in life, especially those things that we have little or no control over.

Trust that can determine whether you allow those feelings to get in your way long term. You have the power to determine how long you allow those feelings to rule you and your future. Here's the thing, even we go through these emotions sometimes, but we have a rule that when a negative feeling hits, we give ourselves a set time to be with the emotion (say 2 to 24 hours) and then return to a better feeling place.

Ways to improve your emotions

- Start each day by choosing how you would like to feel for the rest of the day and what it will take to help you get there
- Choose what vibration you would like to receive and send that out. Imagine what you send out, will come right back to you

- When you are feeling a strong emotion, stop and do not take any action. Strong negative emotions can drive us to do things that we might regret later
- When you feel an emotion that you do not desire, do your best to trace the thought or limiting belief that the emotion came from
- Make a list of activities that make you feel good and inspire you to take action. This could be music, inspirational quotes, motivational speeches etc.
- Choose a positive mantra or affirmation that can counteract the negative thoughts and emotions that you feel, e.g. "every day in every way things are getting better and better"
- When you feel a negative emotion, give yourself a set time to be with it and process the feeling. You can even set an alarm and when it goes off it's time to 'do or die,', time to get out of that space, look in the mirror and remind yourself of the go getter that you really are. Get dressed and show up!

Monitor what you say

Do you know that your tongue is the most powerful organ in your body? Yes, that thing that has no bone and seems to serve little or no purpose, could make you or break you. The things that you say to yourself, in your mind or out loud, could be the tiny margin between if you do some thing or not. Negative self-talk can stop you in your tracks, from going out there and getting the life that you deserve. The only words that should really matter on this journey are the words that you tell yourself. Don't get me wrong, we are not saying not to hear what others have to say, especially those who have you best interest at heart, however, there is a difference between hearing and listening, and the only voice that you should listen to, the only words that should have the ability to make you or break you should be your own words. Speaking to yourself in a positive way is one of the most important tasks that you can do daily.

Gossiping about other people, talking about them in a negative way or making fun of them can also have a negative impact on you. Your unconscious mind does not know that anyone exists outside of you and so the things that you say it takes literally and applies them to you. Also, your unconscious mind does not have a sense of humour and takes the things that you say in jest or as a joke as being real. Despite these things being a limitation of the unconscious mind, if you were to cut out talking about other people and refraining from making jokes at their expense or yours, your mindset and life could be so much better. This can be a challenge, especially when you have people around you who are use to gossiping and making fun of situations and others. Give it a try and you will see over time, how light your life will become as you consciously choose the words you speak and desire to take hold of your life.

Ways to improve what you say

- Keep your internal voice in check, making sure you acknowledge the negative, but don't allow it to take you over
- Make a commitment to only saying what you mean and meaning what you say. Don't make promises that you know you are not going to keep or can't keep
- Learn to say no, sometimes we find this hard and then regret agreeing to things that we do not want to do. Develop the confidence to turn things and people down when it feels right
- Keep your word, when you say things out loud - commit to keeping your word and be a woman of honour. Increasing trust in you
- Complete an inventory of the things you have said to yourself throughout your life, the type of songs you sang or the regular conversations you have had
- Speak positive affirmations over the lives of others; do not wish unkind things on them
- Use positive affirmations out loud to help program your unconscious mind and future thoughts
- Speak the truth, especially if you want others to be honest with you.

Tool #1 The Wheel of Life

What area of life do you need to work on?

Use this process to review different areas of your life to know how well you are doing in each. Every now and again it's a good idea to stop and review where you are. Take some time to assess several different areas, which can help you decide where you should allocate your time and energy.

On a scale of 0-10 grade each area of life,
0 = not doing well
5= doing okay
10 = doing amazing

- Career (work or business)
- Relational (family and friends)
- Relationships (partners and love)
- Social (interests and entertainment)
- Education (learning, skills, capabilities)
- Physical (health, wellbeing and fitness)
- Finances (material possessions)
- Spiritual and personal development

Once you have your scores – choose 2 or three areas that you want to make progress in the most. Write down two or three steps that will help you to get there.

What do you really, really, want!

We live in a world that encourages us to be, do and have more and more, often without having a good idea and understanding of why? Many people are busy doing things and have a focus on what they can get and have in life, when what they are really seeking unconsciously is an experience. For example, if you have a desire to be very wealthy, what is the experience that you believe that wealth will bring to you? More time, more freedom, ability to create opportunities etc. Some of these things can be achieved without the wealth, but we have been socialised to focus on material things rather that the experiences and who we can become. If you have a list of goals or a bucket list, spend some time, exploring why you desire to have these things or experiences.

Make a list of the following…

1. What are the things you desire to be in life?
2. What are the things you desire to do in life?
3. What are the things you desire to have?

What will each of these things allow you to experience? E.g. emotions, thoughts. Can you achieve these experiences without the things you are desiring?

Tool #2 Values Inventory

What is important to you?

If you get to know a person who has achieved success, you're likely to find they are driven to a large extent by a well-defined set of personal values. These are the things that we believe are important to us, which become unconscious drivers and ways for us to evaluate if we are living according to them.

We have values for all areas of our life, including relationships, work, health, learning, fun, family life etc. When we are not living according to our values, this can cause external and internal conflict within us. For example, if you are in a relationship with someone and you value communication, and they don't like to talk about things then, this will be quite difficult. Also, our values can change over time or when there are significant emotional events like a marriage, accident, death, hitting a significant milestone etc. People's values can change at this time, but the difficulty often come, because they are not conscious that their values have changed and the values of the people around them have often stayed the same.

Discovering your values

Step 1. Write down as many words as possible to describe what's important to you in a specific area of life. Start by being as inclusive as possible, writing as many words as you can, around 15-20 for each.

For example, relationship values of.

- Love
- Passion
- Commitment
- Joy and excitement
- Attraction
- Positive communication
- Honesty
- Friendship

Step 2. If you have a lot of words, collapse them words into similar word groups to help you make your list smaller.

Step 3. Pick your top seven values for each area- writing out what they mean and why they are important to you - helping you be clear and concise.

Step 4. Assess how much you are living your top values in each area of your life. Give yourself a score out of 10 for each areas of life and each value. E.g. In career, if freedom is one of your values, how much freedom do you have at work?

0 = no freedom,

5 = some free

10 = total freedom

Tool # 3 Exploring Limiting Beliefs

What limiting or empowering beliefs do you have?

Our beliefs play a big role in determining the quality of our lives, acting as unconscious drivers that shape our attitudes, capabilities and habitual behaviours. The beliefs you have are never absolutely true, as they are not always proven facts; they are more your personal ways of seeing things. Our view of the world is shaped by our perception, which has been developed through our personal experiences and life to date.

How you view other people, experiences, and ourselves, is shaped by what you believe. Beliefs are often seen to be true, especially when there seems to be many other people who have the same belief, or if our belief has not been contested or disproven. However, for every belief you hold, there is always somebody, with a totally opposite view, which they see as being just as valid as yours is to you.

Take some time to explore your unconscious beliefs, as this can help you to understand how you are getting in your own way. To further understand where these beliefs came from, explore the beliefs of the people you grew up around.

Limiting Beliefs

- I can't do this
- I am not good enough
- This is too hard for me
- I don't have enough time
- I am not worthy
- I need more money
- They are better than me
- Good things don't happen to me

Empowering Beliefs

- I can do this
- I am good enough
- I am going to do my very best
- I will make time
- I am worthy
- I have the money that I need and will make more
- They are good at somethings and I have strengths too
- Good things happen to me all the time when I take time to appreciate my life

Tool #4 - Motivational Direction Filter

What is driving you?

Motivation is something that we are considered to have or not, however this tool invites you to look at it in a different way. Motivation can be considered as moving towards or away from something – the things that we believe could cause us pain or pleasure. Tony Robbins is well known for talking about this idea, as he suggests it is helpful to find out whether you are moving towards something because you believe it will please you or away from something because you think it will cause you pain.

Towards Motivation

- Choosing to lose weight because you want to live a healthy life. This is moving towards pleasure and possibilities, which could lead you to be pro-active.
- Wanting to achieve your true potential and success in business, because you want to make a difference in people's lives. Moves you towards something positive and can help with fulfilling your purpose.
- Supporting your family because you know that your contribution will help them to thrive and grow. Moves you toward a healthy vision of them doing well because of your contribution.

Away From Motivation

- If a person chooses to lose weight because they don't want to be considered obese or die, they are moving away from pain. Thus, they are more likely to be inspired by challenges or only when things go wrong.
- Not wanting to fail at something or having things go wrong can inspire you to act in business. However, this can be challenging with a focus on the fear of failure.
- Supporting family because you do not want anything bad to happen to them. This can keep you worrying and anxious even though you are taking action. It can also feel like a heavy burden at times.

Which way is your motivational filter directed?

Knowing the direction of your motivation is important because it will determine your focus and what inspires you to take action. Here are two key questions to help you find out if you are motivated towards or away from...

What do you want in a partner/job/health/____?
What is important to you about a partner/job/your health/__________?

Tool #4 Locus of Control

Where is your locus of control?

It is important to know how you feel about what you do in your life and how it is controlled. The concept of "locus of control" was developed by Julian Rotterin 1954. He suggested your "locus" can either be internal or external.

External locus of control

Do you believe that fate, chance, or a higher being is responsible for running your life?

People with an external locus of control, exhibit less responsibility over their lives. They would always say: if it's meant to be, it's meant to be, believing they have no control over the things that are happening to them, letting external situations influence the outcome of their life. There is a place for allowing and surrender and sometimes letting go and allowing the 'powers that be' to guide and assist us has it's place, however, having a balanced approach is key.

Sometimes people with an external locus of control, worry about the opinions of others and are affected by what other people think, so much so that it can affect their confidence and self-esteem. As we have discussed earlier many women are victims of the thoughts and feelings of other people.

Internal locus of control

Do you believe that whatever happens to you is a result of the choices you make? People with this internal reference take responsibility for the things they do and the results they get, believing that no one else is responsible for their lives. As a result, they have better control of their behaviour and consequently, they attempt to influence others. This can lead to self-reflection and self-inquiry as ways to improve and exceed expectations. Equally, it can lead to being over conscious, self-blaming and critical. Many of us are our own worst self-critic, constantly evaluating every step for faults and mistakes – when done excessively, this can be a barrier to our progress.

Where do you believe you fit on the scale below?

Are you more likely to believe your life is controlled by internal or external forces?

Internal -- External

Which one is better? Well, there's really no definite answer, except that a balance between the two is a good idea to be able to take charge of your life in the right way, at the right time.

LaShartey's Story
My Dream, My Purpose

Growing up I always knew I wanted to help people, women specifically. My dream started out with wanting to be a therapist counseling battered woman and reminding them of how awesome they are. Encouraging them and pulling their gifts to the forefront to be shared with the world. At a young age, no one could tell me that I could not achieve this. That I could not open a wellness centre and write countless books to aid in my purpose. This dream then morphed into wanting to be a life coach and public speaker achieving the same goal of reminding each woman who listens to me, of their inner strength and the power they hold.

As I got older my confidence in being able to live this dream began to dwindle. Life experiences and disappointments began to make me doubt what I was put on the earth to do. I began to learn that not everyone saw me as I saw myself, not everyone recognized my gifts and believed in my purpose. I allowed this to frame how I moved in the world, what I thought of myself and my abilities. That little girl that thought she could conquer the world began to fade into the background and a doubtful, self-conscious woman afraid to fail took her place. I have seen this done too often with women.

We let outside influences affect how we see ourselves or we get so caught up in making sure that everyone around us is lifted and encouraged, that we neglect ourselves. But we are worth seeing our dreams come true, it is very possible to live on purpose and walk in your purpose.

So, tune out the outside distractions and the ones in your own head and let your light shine

Cindy's Story
Surviving

Having always been a strong-willed person it was quite the brutal shock for me to wake up one morning and discover that I was in a long-term relationship with an undiagnosed narcissist. It was the only thing that made sense to me once the dust had settled and I was thinking clearly again. Having been married for over 15 years I thought my life was made. I had what everyone wanted... the husband, the child, the career, a social life, friends, etc. As with all relationships there were ups and downs, but I had always thought that it was part of a marriage... to compromise for the other. But that's the beauty of hindsight; it's only when you look back at your life you can see your short comings, your mistakes and the highs and lows of your life.

For years I was suffering emotionally l, felt low in mood and had suicidal thoughts because I've always felt like I wasn't good enough; that I could not do anything right; and that no matter how hard I try, my actions always made my partner angry or upset. This vicious cycle of me trying, him getting angry, and me feeling a failure became my norm and I could not see it for what it was: toxic. No one knew because I was and have always been a very private person. So, when one day out of the blue I reacted out of the norm, my whole life came tumbling down. This time, my subconscious self said NO! But as you can imagine, old habits die hard. What followed for the next 3 years was a series of me fighting for my mental health while my marriage broke down. I was tearful, blamed myself, begged and pleaded with him and at my lowest tried to take my life, and almost succeeded! It was at that moment I made the conscious decision to leave, but it would turn out that it was not my last. With cycles of being gaslighted, shamed, ridiculed and love bombing I went through a roller coaster of emotions from love to hate to pity and hopelessness.

So, what changed for me? I was blessed to have some of the most amazing women in my life as friends. I have female friends of all ages; all walks of life and they became my support system. One friend in particular has been my emotional and spiritual rock who cried with me, prayed incessantly with and for me and forced me to eat when my body could not stand nutrition. Another friend enlightened me to the type of relationship I was in and helped me joined a Facebook support group for people in abusive relationships. I sought help. From my GP and was placed on anti-depressants and referred for counselling.

Since breaking free from this relationship, I have started my business again and doing well. I am now the proud owner of my very own lash brand along with my Nursing career and beauty business. I have mental freedom and my passport is never dusty.... last year alone I travelled 9 times in the year! And I have amazing friends and family that have come to understand me and the reasons

For my decisions. Was this journey easy? Absolutely not! Is it over? Not by a long shot! But each day I wake up, I thank God for blessing me with such positive support and for being by my side in my darkest moments. I am aware that I can have low periods and together with my counsellor/therapist have devised a plan to help me identify my triggers and have a plan set out that minimises my spiral into darkness. I say affirmations every day and do good deeds; at least one a day to keep me feeling worthy and positive!

So, anyone wondering if they can make it, if they can get out of their situation, can life be better, my answer is YES! You can have a better life for yourself regardless of your financial situation, status, cultural background, etc. What you will need is that hunger to survive, to make your life better, to self-love. When you reach that moment, you will know and nothing can stop you!

"The thing women have yet to learn is nobody gives you power. You just take it."

Roseanne Barr

Chapter 5

Ten Tips to Get Out of Your Way

Getting out of your way is an ongoing process and when you decide to start out on this journey, you may find a few things happen. Making the decision is the first step, yet you may realise that as soon as you do this, there are some things that stick around and become hard to shift - such as behavioural habits that have been with you for a long time and may continue to raise their ugly heads.

Here are some tips to assist you with moving beyond where you are, as taking action is often the most difficult part and you have to persist to overcome the thoughts and emotions that keep holding you back.

Read through each tip and answer the associated questions or complete the exercises. There may be some ideas that require practice and regular implementation, until you fully embedded them, so they become part of your daily experience. More importantly, be patience and kind with yourself, we are not trying to run a race here, but are committed to helping you develop the skills, gifts and resourcefulness required for you to achieve your true potential.

Tip #1 – Self-Inquiry

Self-evaluation is something that you should make a regular practice, so you are aware of what your progress is, knowing if you are on track. This can involve asking yourself thought provoking questions, to investigate personal barriers and learn from experiences. It helps to have the same set of questions that you use at regular intervals, (E.g. weekly monthly quarterly, half yearly and yearly). Doing this at different intervals will allow you to measure where you are at, enabling you to take further actions in a timely manner.

As you know, many people set New Year's resolutions on January 1st and fail. This is because many people do not track their progress and then panic when they notice December has come around and they have achieved little or nothing at all.

Self-evaluation can take place in these areas that make up your daily life.

- Personal relationships
- Personal development
- Health
- Wellbeing and fitness
- Finances
- Spiritual life
- Professional life – career/business
- Social life and entertainment

Here are a few questions to help you understand each area better.

- ✓ How would I grade myself in this area?
- ✓ What are my strengths or weaknesses?
- ✓ What do I want to achieve?
- ✓ Why do I want to achieve these things?
- ✓ What actions have I taken?
- ✓ What actions have I not taken and why not?
- ✓ What outcomes have I achieved?
- ✓ What has prevented me from giving my all to those actions and how can I do better?

Self-inquiry doesn't need to be structured, once you discover the questions that can assist you with understanding yourself, use them on a regular basis in a way that is beneficial to you and takes little time and effort.

Tip #2 Care less, do more

Many believe that it is human nature for women to be nurturing and caring, looking after everyone, putting others before themselves. This can have an impact on how women choose to live their lives, caring what family, friends, colleagues, associates even strangers think about the things they do or don't do. Some of the most common things that are said that can have a negative impact on women are

- When are you going to get married or settle down?
- Don't you think you need to spend more time with your family and looking after your husband?
- You can't have it all, you need to choose between your family or a career
- You need work life balance so you can spend more time with the people that matter

In some scenarios the questions and statements above can be extremely helpful for reflection purposes, however, sometimes these questions make women feel guilty, restricting us from spending our time how we please, and preventing us from putting ourselves first. We can tell you this for sure, you will never please everyone whatever you do and however you do it, someone, somewhere will have something to say about it.

So, in life you must do you, just as long as you are not hurting yourself or anyone else - stay focused and keep it moving. Surround yourself with people who are in your corner, who are pleased with your happiness, and success.

You can achieve this by caring less about the opinion of others, and we know you will continue to treasure those around you. However, be mindful of caring too much to the point that is detrimental to your mental, emotional and physical wellbeing.

Ways to put yourself first

- Stop taking the lessons away from other people, as when you constantly recuse them, they don't always have an opportunity to learn from their mistakes, because you are there to fix things for them
- Make sure that others are ok, but advise how they can make the improvements for themselves, rather than doing it for them
- Spend less time listening to people who just want to have a good moan, gossip, or off load on to you. This can be very draining, especially if this is the main reason, they choose to connect with you. Make yourself less available to them or learn to change the subject, to stay away from this negativity.

Tip# 3 Learning how to prioritise

Do you find yourself constantly saying "I don't have time" or find that you don't have time for you? Always putting yourself on the back burner and other people first? If you are getting in your own way, this will not be because you are not taking action, but because you are busy being mother, wife, daughter, sister, friend and everything in between. Your to do lists might be as long as your arm, and you feel there are not enough hours in the day to get through everything.

Time management and how you organise your day is key to getting things done. As a woman you are expected to juggle many balls, and prioritising with the help of a few tips and tricks can be your best asset.

- A daily, weekly or monthly "To Do List" can help you to stay focused and know that tasks you need to complete. There are many apps that enable you to create lists, or you can simply create them in your notes, or hand write them
- Target the things that are both urgent and important for you to complete, as this will help you with getting the most important things done first, especially if you keep putting them off.
- A timed planner would help you plot out your day, including how long it takes you to do certain tasks
- Tackle the most challenging things first, as it's easy to do the things that you enjoy opposed to doing the things that you need to get done
- Be intentional when setting your daily tasks and take lots of action on the days when you feel you have the most energy, as you do not know how you will feel the day after.
- Review your method of prioritising on a quarterly basis to see if it is still effective and it's working for you. If you find that you are not sticking to things,

find another method to give you a fresh perspective and boost.

- Think about setting just three things that you would like to get through each day, some people call these Most Important Tasks (MITs). Make it your mission to get through them and tick them off your list.
- Most importantly, don't be afraid of saying NO, but be more concerned about stretching yourself thin and not giving your best.

Tip# 4 Muscles Memory – create good feelings

One of the things that stops us from taking action are the negative feelings we experience when we think about difficult tasks or challenges. These feelings can completely railroad us and put us off, while contributing to our fears. Our muscles have a memory, which serves us by remembering how to do things. Muscle memory is often created through repetition, until a new habit is formed. However, significant emotional events can create a memory in our muscles especially if trauma has been experienced. For a moment, think about something that you have tasted or would not consider tasting that when you think about it, your body has a reaction. This is muscles memory, as the reaction is stored within the unconscious mind, as a protective measure, should you experience the same phenomena in the future.

Despite this serving a necessary purpose for survival reasons, this can work against us. For example, if you have failed at something in the past or have had a bad experience, you may have developed an unconscious memory, no matter how slight that prevents you from having the same experience again. The challenge here is that even though this protective measure has been developed to keep you safe, it also keeps you in your comfort zone.

Only taking action when you feel like it or when you feel good, can be counterproductive, especially when you are going through challenging times or when things get tough. It is inevitable that as you make progress in life, obstacles will turn up and learning to take action even when you don't feel like it, can be the difference between success and failure. The most successful entrepreneurs will tell you that taking action during tough times, is crucial to ensure things get done.

Pro-actively creating positive habits helps to build positive muscle memories, which are necessary for those times when you are struggling. As there will be times when you feel like you are letting yourself or others down, when you feel like you are not performing at your best, or when you want to give up. The good news is, there are several things that you can do to create feel good feelings, to counteract these moments.

- Create a morning ritual, where you prepare yourself for the day ahead. Keep it short and sweet, affirming that the day will be great and that anything that happens will provide you with an opportunity to learn and grow.
- Having a playlist of feel good music is a good way to lift a low mood and set you up for the day a head. Music has been called food for the soul, as it can take us to a good place and when you add a little dance, the positive emotions start to flow even more.
- Repeating daily affirmations help to focus our minds and over time if said repetitively, start to become embedded in the unconscious mind. Why not start with 'Today is a good day!'
- Gratitude logs enable you to identify and write down the things that you appreciate in life. Taking time to acknowledge and remember these things can help to put life into perspective, especially when you are not having a great day.
- Volunteering for a cause assists you to make a contribution to the life of others, making a difference a long the way. Being of service is a noble thing to do and can make you feel good about yourself as someone that has moral purpose.
- Hobbies which challenge you, but you enjoy can take you way from the doom and gloom or repetitive nature of life. Find and pursue a hobby

that takes you away from thinking about all that needs to get done and spend time enjoying something that you do for the fun of it.

- Visualisation exercises can either be done in the mind or you can create a vision board. Some might refer to this as daydreaming but it's a good way to focus on what you desire to be, do and have - inspiring you to take action towards what you want.
- Prayer helps us to have faith that we are not alone and that there is always love, guidance and assistance available to us.

Tip# 5 - Get an accountability partner

When you set yourself goals make them real by writing them down with an action plan is the first step and you could stop there. However, one of the problems is that when we keep goals to our self, there is a danger that you could just not get things done. Let's face it, no one but you knows, yet this could be slowing your own progress and hindering your success. An accountability partner is someone who you give permission to…

- check that you are completing your goals
- challenge you to take action and stick to your plan

- ask you those hard questions when it comes what might be getting in your way
- encourage and motivate you on the days when you feel low or when things become too much
- give you a wake-up call when things are not going in the direction you have planned
- help remind you of your focus, vision and mission

It's about having someone who knows what you want to achieve, someone that you trust, who you know has your back and feels no way in challenging you to do what needs to be done with care and a positive intention. Also, by having someone there it makes it harder for things to fall through the cracks, because let's face it, it is harder to lie to someone who you trust and trusts you, than it is to lie to yourself. It is important that you also understand what an accountability partner is not…

- a person who will do things for you
- a mentor to give you the right advice you need to help you take the right actions
- a coach to help you overcome barriers
- an employee who will take on the tasks you don't want to do

Despite this if you have a good accountability partner, with some great skills they can be an excellent sounding board, who can help guide and advise you. You must also be able to do the same, as there is no use giving all that you can, but you don't receive any value in return. Choose wisely!

Tip# 6 Come off social media

Although Social Media has become the go to place for keeping in touch with others or for business, there is also a negative side to engaging on these platforms. Social Media has become the place where most people put the best parts of their daily lives while leaving out the not so good bits. This can give a false sense of what the world is really like and it could also lead you to compare yourself to others, measuring your progress by their standards, when in fact you are comparing yourself to something that may have been inflated. This practice could lead to a decline in your mental health, as you might end up feeling that…

- you have not achieved as much as others
- you are not as beautiful, slim or good looking
- your life is not as calm, rosy or together
- you have not succeeded enough and need to achieve more

Apart from unhelpful comparisons, have you ever tried to think about how much time you waste scrolling through social media? Hours that could have been spent being more productive. Social Media is not all bad, however when you are not getting things done, it's important to take breaks and learn how to be more present in the moment. Thus, spend time detoxing from the cyber world and focus on the task at hand.

Here are a few tips to help:

- Turn notifications off on your phone for all social media platforms
- Have a set time when you go onto social media and for how long
- Have a day when you stay away and invest that time into something else
- Go onto social media knowing that everything that you see on there is not necessarily the truth
- At least once a week make time and use other forms of communication, to contact friends and family like a good old telephone chat or house visit
- Delete, unfollow or mute negative people and stories
- Follow and engage with positive people

Tip# 7 Trackers

Trackers are one of the most useful tools to help you stay on track. Like with goals and having an accountability partner, trackers are there as a visual aid to keep you accountable. You can use trackers for a variety of purposes or projects as they are a good strategy of seeing where you are at any given point.

Trackers are good for...

- Practicing self-discipline, as you develop a consistent approach and way of completing tasks
- Staying focused - so you know what actions need to be done, and how many times a day or week
- Creating new habits - starting a new habit to replace an old one, will help you get better results quicker e.g. tracking how many times you chose to chew gum, rather than how many times you decided not to smoke a cigarette.
- Keeping you inspired - monitoring your success and distance travel can keep you wanting to take more action, even on the days when you do not feel like it.

Don't just leave it to your memory, create a visual way of knowing how you are progressing and therefore giving yourself a better chance of success. Here are a few things to think about before deciding on how and what to track.

- Choose a small number of things to keep track of - having too many different things that you want to improve or change, can make you feel de-motivated if it becomes too difficult to stay consistent
- Make sure you have the resources that you need to help you along the way, e.g. do you need a water bottle that helps you track your water intake easily?

can you purchase gym equipment that can be used at home?

- Think about the tools that can help you - do you need a daily planner, download an app, tracker chart etc? Whatever you use make sure it is easily accessible so you can record how you are doing
- Join a group or get other people on board who are tracking the same things as you. This can help to keep you motivated and inspired to do well

Tip# 8 Affirmations

Affirmations are positive statements that you can say in your mind or out loud, as a way of declaring something that you believe or would like to be true. What you say does not need to be true yet, however, affirmations can offer emotional support or encouragement for the things that you would like to achieve.

These statements or phrases allow you to declare positive things, ways of being, experiences or material possessions, but can also be used to get rid of negative though patterns. Practicing daily affirmations can be a source of reassurance, that you can do the things that you have set out for yourself.

When writing affirmations:

- They should always be written in the present tense and first person. I am.......... I choose.... I declare....... I affirm that....
- They should be a regular practice and should not only be used when you find yourself in a difficult position
- Do your best to remember them and when writing your own make them short and concise
- They should be in line with the goals and the opposite to any negative thoughts or limiting beliefs that you are experiencing.
- Write affirmations that help you become the type of person that you desire

It is a great practice to have affirmations as part of your morning ritual. They set you up for the day ahead and they also help you to be motivated. Revisiting your affirmations during the day will help you to keep a good vibration and mood. When begin to say affirmations to yourself, you may find that you do not believe them at first and it may seem like you are just reciting words. The psychology behind saying them on a regular basis is that anything that is repeated consistently, over a long period of time at regular intervals, becomes embedded into the unconscious mind. Also, the unconscious mind is not able to discriminate between what is real and what we make up. Remember the more you say the affirmations the more you will believe them.

Tip# 9 Meditation

We spend most of our working life thinking, non-stop thinking, thinking, thinking! We are human thinking machines, yes I said the word think again, to represent just how much time we spend in our heads. Being without thoughts for some can seem scary, yet once you try it you might discover a sense of freedom and inner peace.

Taking time away from your thoughts can assist you with

- Clearing your mind from the constant train of thoughts
- Creating a sense of inner peace within, that you can choose to access using simple techniques
- Freeing yourself from negative emotions that can consume you
- Enables you to gain clarity when focusing on something specific

Meditation is increasing in popularity and there are a range of resources to assist you with the learning techniques and implementing practices. Keep tips when meditating

- Be kind to yourself, allowing your thoughts to come and go - when starting out the aim is not to be completely without thought
- Become an observer of your thoughts, watching as they come and go, placing them into a bubble so they float away

- Set yourself a challenge to meditate at the same time each day and when you start out, think about doing a 10, 21 or 30 day challenge
- Find a good position for you to sit in, one that allows you to be comfortable for the duration of your session and avoid lying down as you are likely to fall asleep
- If you are trying hard to meditate you are trying too hard. Learn to go with the flow and see what happens.

Meditation is no longer reserved for monks, sages and gurus and is available and accessible to us all. Take time to learn the basic techniques, while adapting them to suit your lifestyle and needs.

Tip# 10 Develop a purpose and passion

Have you ever heard the saying "Do something that you love, and you will never work another day in your life?" Your passion is the compelling emotion that supports and drives your dreams, whereas your purpose is your deeper reason for your existence - the Why? Knowing what your purpose is helps to give you a sense of fulfilment, inspiring you to live a happier and healthier lifestyle. Not only that, but scientific research has shown that having a purpose also leads to several health benefits and better sleep. A few ways in which you can discover your purpose and passion is by:

- Looking at what gets you out of bed in the morning?
- What sets your soul on fire?
- Looking at what you would do regardless of whether you are rewarded or not?
- Considering what you would continue to do even if you did not have to?
- What do people say about you? What do they appreciate?
- What have you been through that you have learned key lessons from and how can you pass that on to others?
- What community or practice do you get lost in, and time seems to go too quickly?
- What gives you the greatest joy and seems to come easy to you when others may find it difficult?

Your passion is what drives your purpose, as a deep desire to wake up every day and do what you love. It is also important to have a WHY? What would you like to be remembered for? There's no point waking up every day and doing things that you are not passionate about, as doing this whether for money, love or fame, can lead to a life where you are just existing and not living - making life a chore. And yes, it's possible to turn your purpose and passion into profit and enjoy both worlds.

"Think like a queen. A queen is not afraid to fail. Failure is another stepping stone to greatness."

Oprah Winfrey

Hermilyns' Story
Leaving Paradise

I was born in the beautiful Island of Grenada, where I obtained my formative upbringing. However, it was in the summer months of 1989, I migrated to the USA. I still remember my last drive to the airport. I started to take mental pictures of the houses, the people, roads and the atmosphere. Somehow, I knew this going to be my last drive through the area and it would be years before I see my beloved Grenada again. When I got to the states, I had my dream of going back to school, getting my degree, married and live in a huge house somewhere in the US. Who knew it would take me 15 years before half of my dreams to come true?

I was young, naïve, experienced and emotionally vulnerable. I became wrapped up in a man that I loved. He was dark smooth chocolaty, strikingly tall and handsome man. His personality, he was quite shy, so I took the lead or being the forward one, letting him know that I was very interested. Shortly thereafter, I became pregnant, and things were going great, well to me. Until, one summer day in 1996 he surprisingly slapped me because I was in no mood to open the door for him. He had keys! I was shocked because I thought I vetted him well in the domestic abuse area. I could not believe he hit me! He quickly apologized, and I forgave him, and things went back to normal or, so I thought. The baby arrived, and an entire new issue arose. He was overtly jealous of the baby, which I mentioned to a few people and they assured me that it was normal. But it did not. It got worse and I spent the next 6 years trying to balance my love for him and my love for the baby.

I refrained from telling anyone, who would believe me when there were no visible marks on my body? Would you have believed ME? When I did confided in certain family members but instead I was greeted with responses, such as Hermie, you have to behave yourself, for he is a good catch, don't you dare tell family secrets, a little licks or beating won't hurt and so on and so forth. (Re-phrased)

I stayed for 6 years because I wanted to be married and he knew that, I did not want to be a single mother. BUT…It was the summer of 2002 I had enough an incident happened where he threatened my life and I made the decision that I needed to get out.

Step 1: I made a decision. It is not as simple as it sounds, but it's a decision you will make.

Step 2: Create a plan. I started a save most of my earnings. I copied all important documents, pay stubs, birth certificates, Social security number, tax documents, proof of citizenship, police reports. Hide all documents somewhere safe. Make and go over any emergency plans with your children and a trusted family.

Step 3: Journal Everything. Write every detail down, save text messages, emails and phone calls.

When I got out, I started selling jewellery on the street of Brooklyn, the online. I went back to school obtained my bachelor's degree in Business Management, graduated Magna cum laude in 2013 and Cum laude in 2014. In 2015 I moved to Texas with my boys.

Now my goal is to create awareness and resources to Domestic Violence Victims and Survivors throughout the Caribbean and the US. In addition, to creating awareness, my goal is to empower strengthens, and uplift Domestic Violence survivors by helping them regain their self-esteem and encourage self-sufficiency through online workshops.

Sarah's Story
Self-care is a Self Must

"I'm done." Two words that changed my life forever as I watched the man, I loved breakdown and cry. They say all you need is love but it's just not as simple as that.

When I met him, it was all so easy. On our second date as he drove away, we both cried.

We moved in together within a few months and everything was great then his moods started to change. My life became centred around the man I loved, the man who spent most of his life feeling broken or as the doctors call it bi-polar. His dark days, his bright days and the fluctuations of them. It got worse after my dad died. I questioned every part of my life, my legacy and my impact on this world.

If he was happy, we were happy.

If he was down, we were down.

If he was angry, I was scared.

Our relationship was driven by the chemicals in his brain, but we loved each other, right? I found the one.

As I stood in front of him that day, I shattered inside as I said "I'm done. I'm sorry, love isn't enough."

Self-care is about self-love. It's about learning who the f you are, knowing who the real you is and learning to love that person, that spirit, that soul before anyone else. Love for others isn't enough. Love for yourself is as important as water and food.

Self-care is not selfish. It's a self must!

Notes

Dionne is a serial founder, podcast host and coach, who is trained in neuro-linguistic programming, timeline therapy and hypnosis. Dionne gets to the root cause(s) of what is holding individuals back, uncovering personal barriers and unconscious drivers.

Dionne Jude
www.mybusinesslinks.co/dionnejude

Niasha is the founder and CEO of Divas Empowered Network, a coaching service where she helps women find and build their confidence from inside out, so that they can start living a life of abundance and stop living a life of self-lack.

Niasha Toole Keens-Douglas
www.onelinkup.co/divasempowerednetwork

Contributors

Zephorah Nuré

wwww.zephorahnure.com

Instagram @enchantresszephorah

Dr Yvette Ankrah

www.yvetteankrah.com

Instagram @yvette.ankrah

Djennicia Francis

Instagram @ speak_peek_childrens_books

Nicole Freeman-Kirkland

Instagram @bythenumberzcpa

Facebook @bythenumberzcpa

Dr Gwen Martin

Instagram @drgwenscounselorcafe

Marchell Coleman

Instgram @marchellcoleman

LaShartey Mcghee

www.my-truly.beautiful.com

Cindy Mollineau

Instagram @cbmlashes, @cbm.makeup

Hermilyn Marryshow

www.facebook.com/groups/380131675919411

Sarah Shard

Instagram @inspiredlifeclub

Printed in Great Britain
by Amazon

43670492R00064